Impressum
Verlag: BABADADA GmbH, Nedderfeld 112 , 22529 Hamburg
Geschäftsführer / Verlagsleitung: Harald Hof
Druck: Books on Demand GmbH, In de Tarpen 42, 22848 Norderstedt

Imprint
Publisher: BABADADA GmbH, Nedderfeld 112 , 22529 Hamburg, Germany
Managing Director / Publishing direction: Harald Hof
Print: Books on Demand GmbH, In de Tarpen 42, 22848 Norderstedt

5ch00l

school

cl455r00m
classroom

d1v1d3
divide

186/2

b04rd
board

5ch00l y4rd
school yard

734ch3r
teacher

p4p3r
paper

wr173
write

p3n
pen

d35k
desk

rul3r
ruler

b00k
book

pup1l
pupil

547ch3l

satchel

p3nc1l c453

pencil case

p3nc1l

pencil

p3nc1l 5h4rp3n3r

pencil sharpener

rubb3r

rubber

dr4w1n6 p4d

drawing pad

dr4w1n6

drawing

p41n7bru5h

paintbrush

p41n7 b0x

paint box

5c1550r5

scissors

6lu3

glue

3x3rc153 b00k

exercise book

h0m3w0rk

homework

numb3r

number

2+2

4dd

add

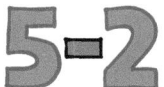

5ub7r4c7

subtract

mul71ply

multiply

c4lcul473

calculate

l3773r

letter

4lph4b37

alphabet

w0rd

word

73x7

text

r34d

read

ch4lk

chalk

l3550n

lesson

r361573r

register

3x4m1n4710n

exam

c3r71f1c473

certificate

5ch00l un1f0rm

school uniform

3duc4710n

education

3ncycl0p3d14

encyclopedia

un1v3r517y

university

m1cr05c0p3

microscope

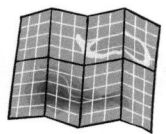

m4p

map

w4573-p4p3r b45k37

waste-paper basket

7r4v3l

travel

h073l
hotel
Grand
h0573l
hostel
ROOMS
CHANGE
curr3ncy 3xch4n63 0ff1c3
bureau de change
5u17c453
suitcase
c4r
car

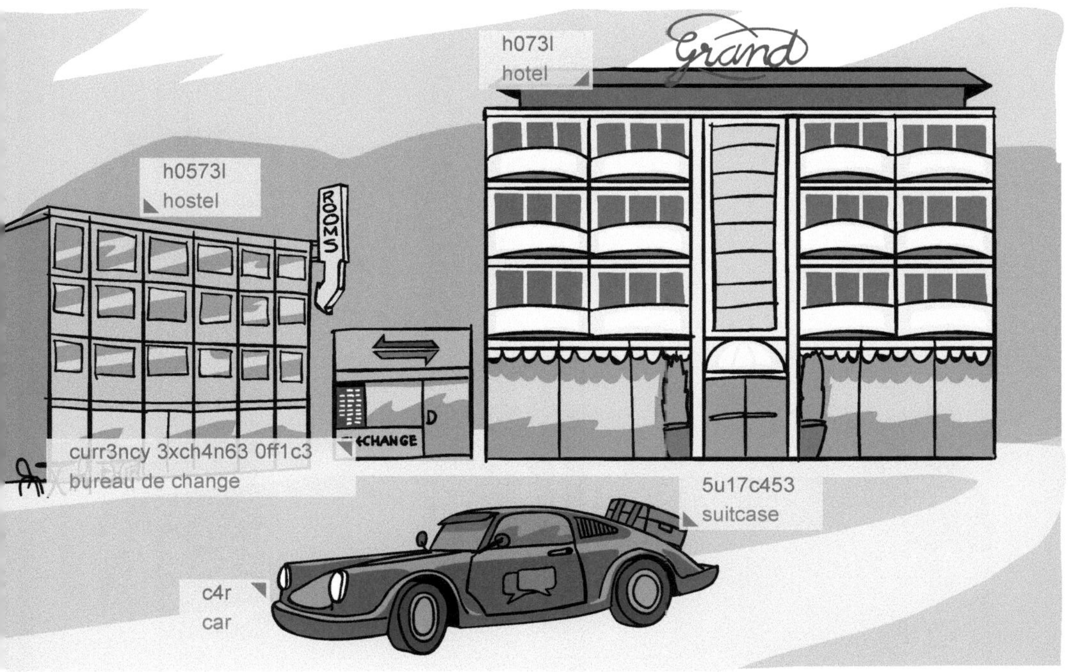

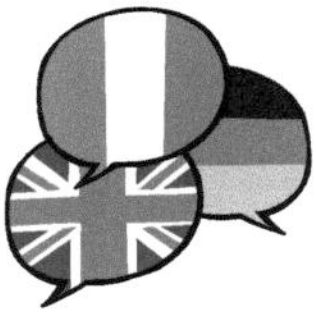

l4n6u463

language

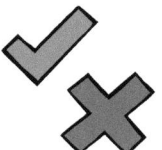

y35 / n0

yes / no

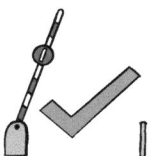

0k4y

Okay

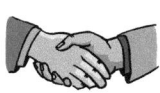

h3ll0

hello

7r4n5l470r

translator

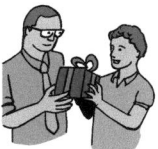

7h4nk y0u

Thank you

h0w much 15

how much is…?

1 d0 n07 und3r574nd

I do not understand

pr0bl3m

problem

600d 3v3n1n6!

Good evening!

600d m0rn1n6!

Good morning!

600d n16h7!

Good night!

600dby3

bye bye

d1r3c710n

direction

lu66463

luggage

b46

bag

b4ckp4ck

backpack

6u357

guest

r00m

room

5l33p1n6 b46

sleeping bag

73n7

tent

70ur157 1nf0rm4710n

tourist information

b34ch

beach

cr3d17 c4rd

credit card

br34kf457

breakfast

lunch

lunch

d1nn3r

dinner

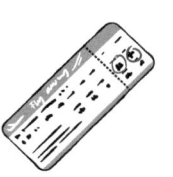

71ck37

ticket

3l3v470r

lift

574mp

stamp

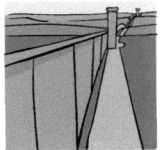

b0rd3r

border

cu570m5

customs

3mb455y

embassy

v154

visa

p455p0r7

passport

7r4n5p0r7

transport

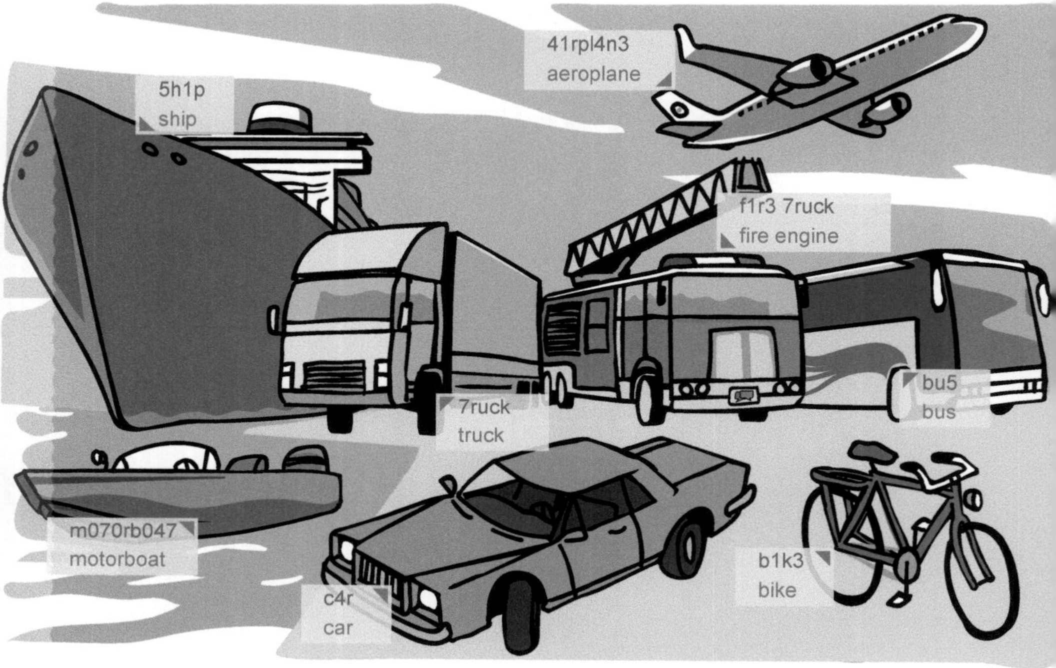

41rpl4n3
aeroplane
5h1p
ship
f1r3 7ruck
fire engine
7ruck
truck
bu5
bus
m070rb047
motorboat
c4r
car
b1k3
bike

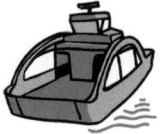

f3rry
ferry

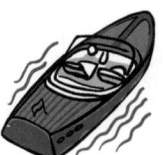

b047
boat

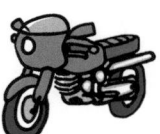

m070rb1k3
motorbike

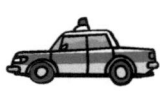

p0l1c3 c4r
police car

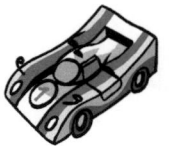

r4c1n6 c4r
racing car

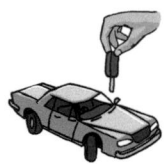

r3n74l c4r
rental car

c4r 5h4r1n6

car sharing

70w 7ruck

breakdown truck

64rb463 7ruck

refuse truck

3n61n3

motor

fu3l

fuel

fu3l 574710n

petrol station

7r4ff1c 516n

traffic sign

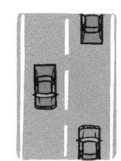

7r4ff1c

traffic

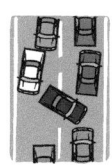

7r4ff1c j4m

traffic jam

p4rk1n6 l07

car park

7r41n 574710n

train station

7r4ck5

tracks

7r41n

train

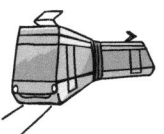

7r4m

tram

w460n

carriage

h3l1c0p73r

helicopter

41rp0r7

airport

70w3r

tower

p4553n63r

passenger

c0n741n3r

container

c4r70n

carton

c4r7

cart

b45k37

basket

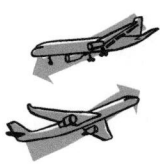

74k3 0ff / l4nd

take off / land

c17y

city

v1ll463

village

c17y c3n73r

city centre

h0u53

house

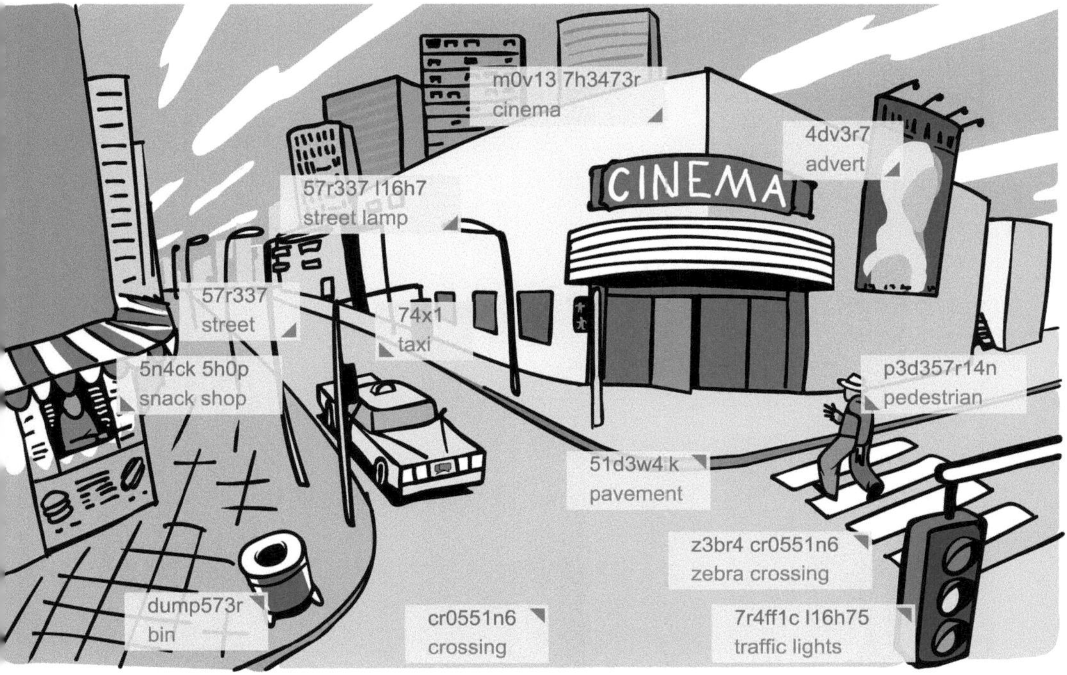

m0v13 7h3473r
cinema

4dv3r7
advert

57r337 l16h7
street lamp

CINEMA

57r337
street

74x1
taxi

p3d357r14n
pedestrian

5n4ck 5h0p
snack shop

51d3w4 k
pavement

z3br4 cr0551n6
zebra crossing

dump573r
bin

cr0551n6
crossing

7r4ff1c l16h75
traffic lights

hu7

hut

4p4r7m3n7

flat

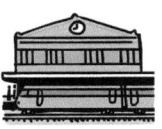

7r41n 574710n

train station

c17y h4ll

town hall

mu53um

museum

5ch00l

school

un1v3r517y

university

b4nk

bank

h05p174l

hospital

h073l

hotel

ph4rm4cy

pharmacy

0ff1c3

office

b00k 5h0p

book shop

5h0p

shop

fl0w3r 5h0p

florist's

5up3rm4rk37

supermarket

m4rk37

market

d3p4r7m3n7 570r3

department store

f15hm0n63r'5 5h0p

fishmonger's

m4ll

shopping centre

h4rb0r

harbour

p4rk

park

b3nch

bench

br1d63

bridge

5741r5

stairs

5ubw4y

underground

7unn3l

tunnel

bu5 570p

bus stop

b4r

bar

r3574ur4n7

restaurant

p057b0x

postbox

57r337 516n

street sign

p4rk1n6 m373r

parking meter

z00

zoo

5w1mm1n6 p00l

swimming pool

m05qu3

mosque

f4rm
farm

p0llu710n
pollution

c3m373ry
graveyard

church
church

pl4y6r0und
playground

73mpl3
temple

l4nd5c4p3
landscape

l34f
leaf

516np057
signpost

p47h
way

m34d0w
meadow

570n3
stone

7r33
tree

h1k3r
hiker

r1v3r
river

6r455
grass

fl0w3r
flower

v4ll3y
valley

h1ll
hill

l4k3
lake

f0r357
forest

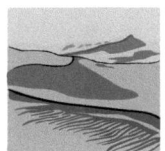

d353r7
desert

v0lc4n0
volcano

c457l3
castle

r41nb0w
rainbow

mu5hr00m
mushroom

p4lm 7r33
palm tree

m05qu170
mosquito

fly
fly

4n7
ant

b33
bee

5p1d3r
spider

b337l3

beetle

fr06

frog

5qu1rr3l

squirrel

h3d63h06

hedgehog

h4r3

hare

0wl

owl

b1rd

bird

5w4n

swan

b04r

boar

d33r

deer

m0053

moose

d4m

dam

w1nd 7urb1n3

wind turbine

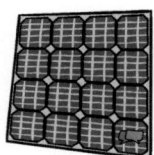

50l4r p4n3l

solar panel

cl1m473

climate

r3574ur4n7
restaurant

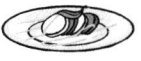

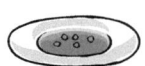

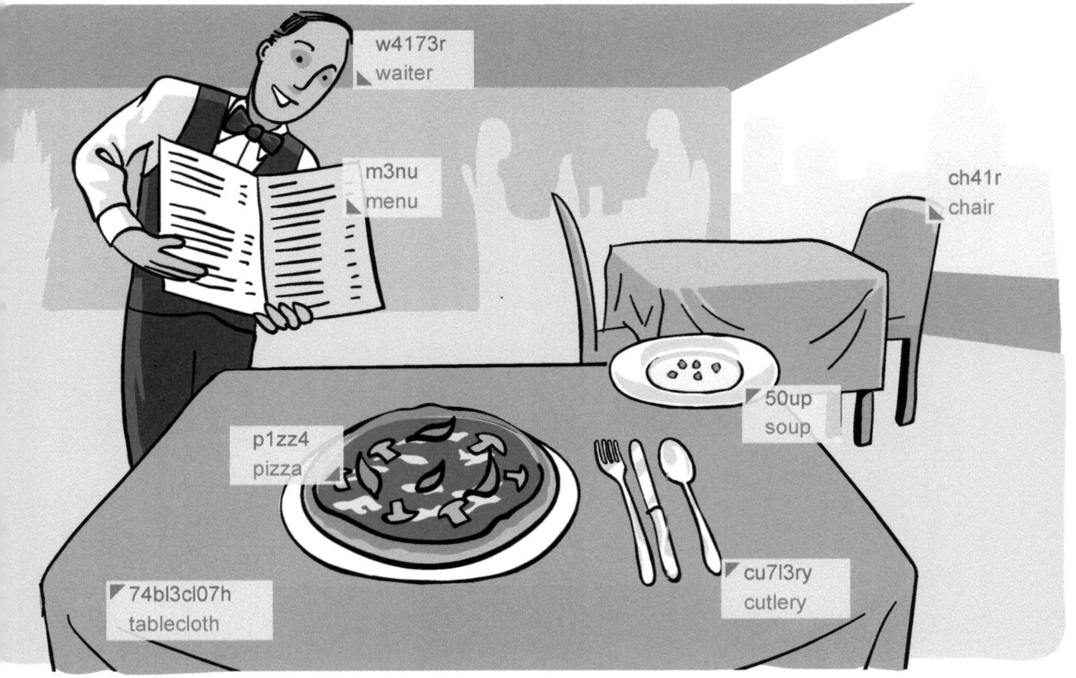
w4173r
waiter
m3nu
menu
ch41r
chair
50up
soup
p1zz4
pizza
cu7l3ry
cutlery
74bl3cl07h
tablecloth

574r73r
....
starter

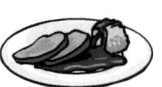

m41n c0ur53
....
main course

d3553r7
....
dessert

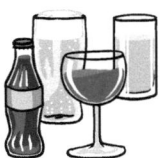

dr1nk5
....
drinks

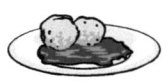

f00d
....
food

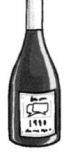

b077l3
....
bottle

f457 f00d
....
fast food

57r337 f00d
....
street food

734p07
....
teapot

5u64r b0wl
....
sugar bowl

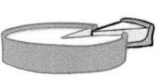

p0r710n
....
portion

35pr3550 m4ch1n3
....
espresso machine

h16h ch41r
....
high chair

b1ll
....
bill

7r4y
....
tray

kn1f3
....
knife

f0rk
....
fork

5p00n
....
spoon

7345p00n
....
teaspoon

53rv13773
....
serviette

6l455
....
glass

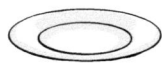

pl473

plate

50up pl473

soup plate

54uc3r

saucer

54uc3

sauce

54l7 5h4k3r

salt pot

p3pp3r m1ll

pepper mill

v1n364r

vinegar

01l

oil

5p1c35

spices

k37chup

ketchup

mu574rd

mustard

m4y0nn4153

mayonnaise

5up3rm4rk37

supermarket

5p3c14l 0ff3r
special offer
FOR
cu570m3r
customer
d41ry pr0duc75
dairy
fru17
fruit
5h0pp1n6 c4r7
trolley

BUTCHERS

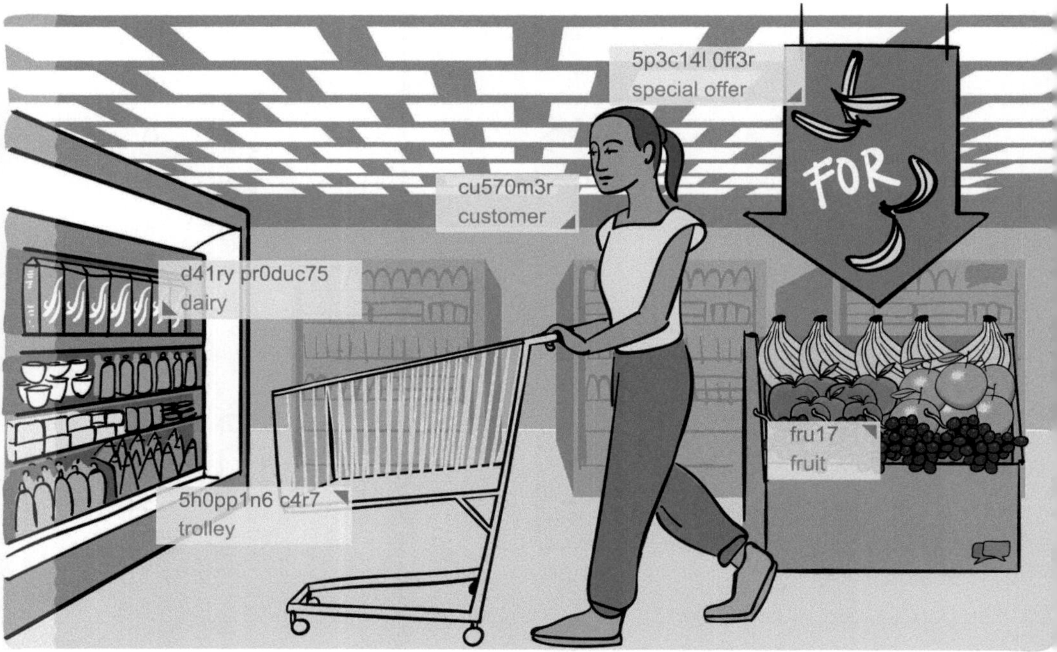

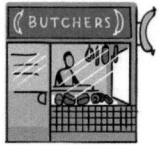

bu7ch3r'5 5h0p

butcher´s

BAKERY

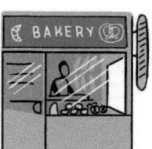

b4k3ry

baker´s

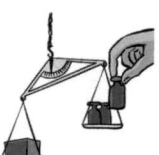

w316h

weigh

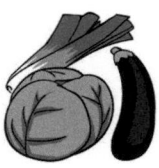

v36374bl35

vegetables

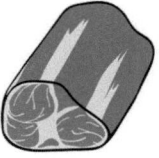

m347

meat

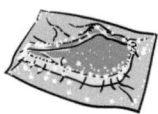

fr0z3n f00d

frozen food

c0ld cu75

cold meat

c4nn3d f00d

tinned food

d373r63n7

washing powder

c4ndy

sweets

h0u53h0ld pr0duc75

household products

cl34n1n6 pr0duc75

cleaning products

54l35 r3pr353n7471v3

salesperson

c45h r361573r

till

c45h13r

cashier

5h0pp1n6 l157

shopping list

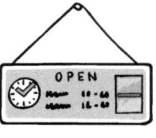

0p3n1n6 h0ur5

opening hours

w4ll37

wallet

cr3d17 c4rd

credit card

b46

bag

pl4571c b46

plastic bag

drinks

w473r

water

ju1c3

juice

m1lk

milk

c0k3

coke

w1n3

wine

b33r

beer

4lc0h0l

alcohol

c0c04

cocoa

734

tea

c0ff33

coffee

35pr3550

espresso

c4ppucc1n0

cappuccino

b4n4n4

banana

4ppl3

apple

0r4n63

orange

m3l0n

melon

l3m0n

lemon

c4rr07

carrot

64rl1c

garlic

b4mb00

bamboo

0n10n

onion

mu5hr00m

mushroom

nu75

nuts

n00dl35

noodles

5p46h3771

spaghetti

r1c3

rice

54l4d

salad

fr135

chips

fr13d p0747035

fried potatoes

p1zz4

pizza

h4mbur63r

hamburger

54ndw1ch

sandwich

35c4l0p3

cutlet

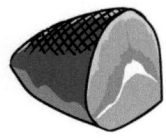

h4m

ham

54l4m1

salami

54u5463

sausage

ch1ck3n

chicken

r0457

roast

f15h

fish

p0rr1d63 0475

porridge oats

mu35l1

muesli

c0rnfl4k35

cornflakes

fl0ur

flour

cr01554n7

croissant

br34d r0ll

bread roll

br34d

bread

70457

toast

c00k135

biscuits

bu773r

butter

curd

curd

c4k3

cake

366

egg

fr13d 366

fried egg

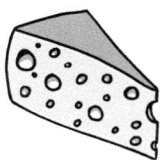

ch3353

cheese

1c3 cr34m

ice cream

5u64r

sugar

h0n3y

honey

j3lly

jam

n0u647 cr34m

chocolate spread

curry

curry

f4rm
farm

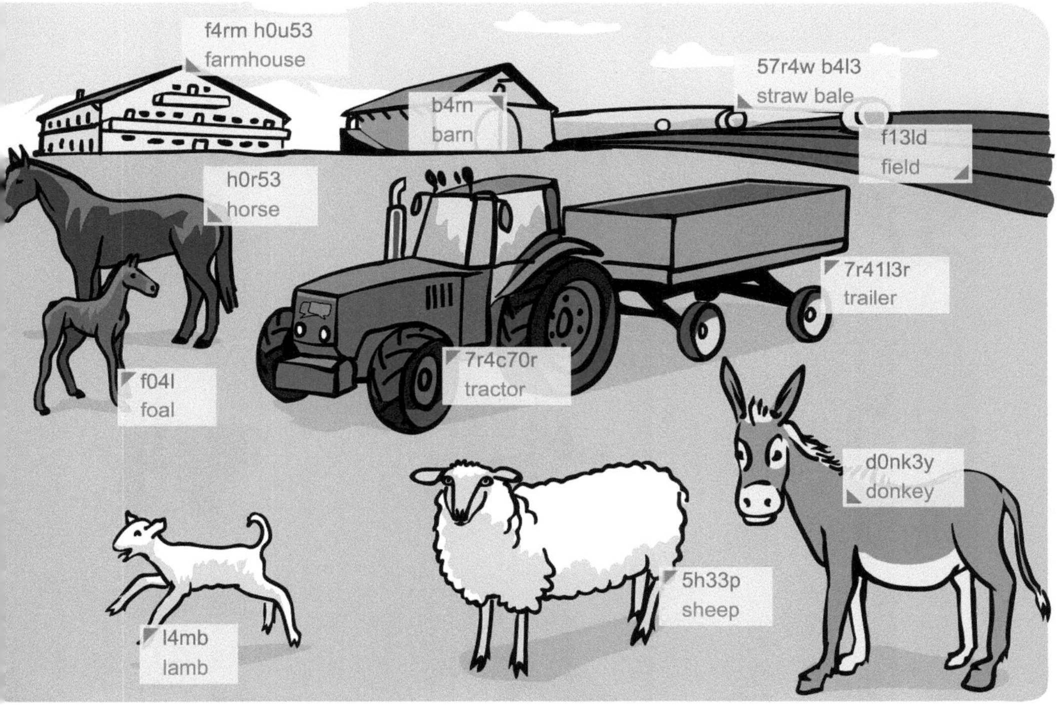
f4rm h0u53
farmhouse
b4rn
barn
57r4w b4l3
straw bale
f13ld
field
h0r53
horse
7r41l3r
trailer
f04l
foal
7r4c70r
tractor
d0nk3y
donkey
5h33p
sheep
l4mb
lamb

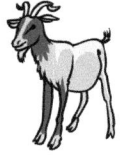

6047

goat

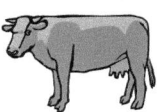

c0w

cow

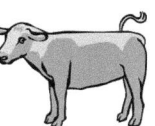

c4lf

calf

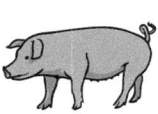

p16

pig

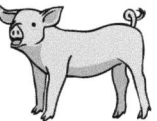

p16l37

piglet

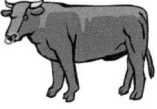

bull

bull

60053

goose

duck

duck

ch1ck

chick

h3n

hen

c0ck3r3l

cock

r47

rat

c47

cat

m0u53

mouse

0x

ox

d06

dog

d06 h0u53

doghouse

64rd3n h053

garden hose

w473r1n6 c4n

watering can

5cy7h3

scythe

pl0u6h

plough

f4rm - farm

51ckl3

sickle

h03

hoe

p17chf0rk

pitchfork

4x3

axe

pu5hc4r7

wheelbarrow

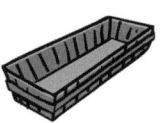

7r0u6h

trough

m1lk c4n

milk can

54ck

sack

f3nc3

fence

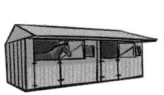

574bl3

stable

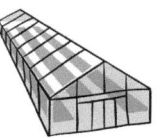

6r33nh0u53

greenhouse

501l

soil

533d

seed

f3r71l1z3r

fertilizer

c0mb1n3 h4rv3573r

combine harvester

h4rv357

harvest

h4rv357

harvest

y4m5

yams

wh347

wheat

50y4

soy

p07470

potato

c0rn

corn

r4p3533d

rapeseed

fru17 7r33

fruit tree

m4n10c

cassava

6r41n

cereals

h0u53

house

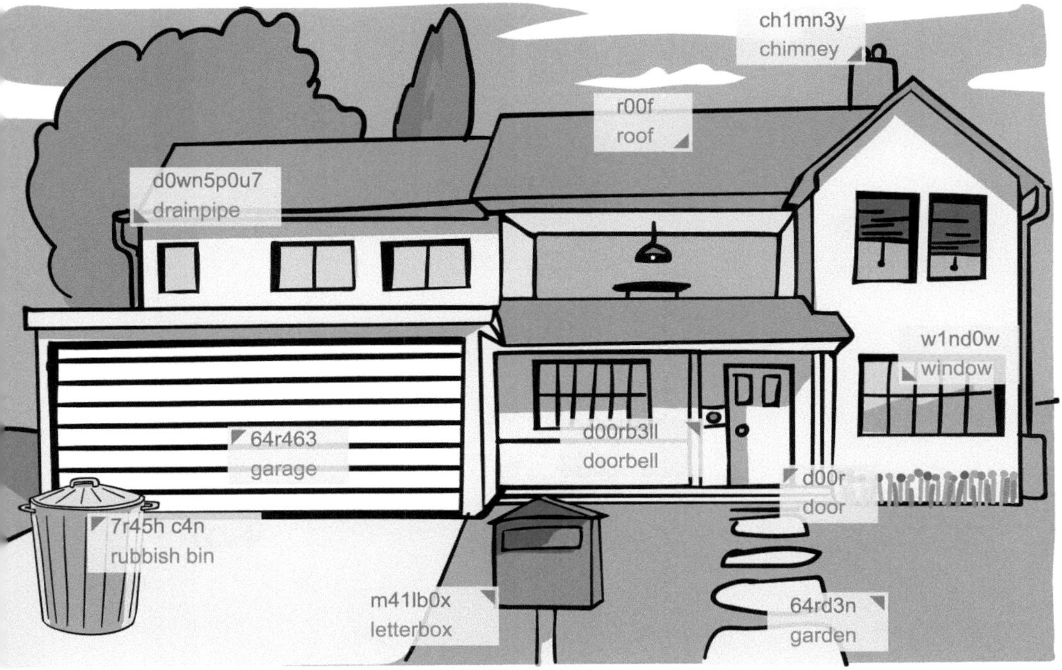
ch1mn3y
chimney
r00f
roof
d0wn5p0u7
drainpipe
w1nd0w
window
64r463
garage
d00rb3ll
doorbell
d00r
door
7r45h c4n
rubbish bin
m41lb0x
letterbox
64rd3n
garden

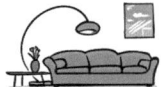

l1v1n6 r00m

living room

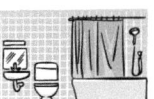

b47hr00m

bathroom

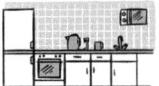

k17ch3n

kitchen

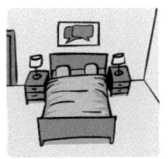

b3dr00m

bedroom

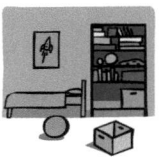

ch1ld'5 r00m

child's room

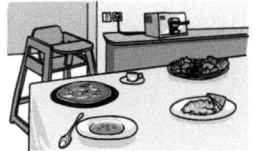

d1n1n6 r00m

dining room

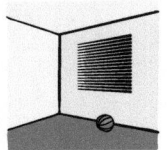

fl00r

floor

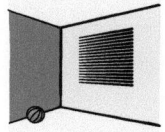

w4ll

wall

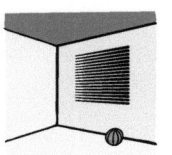

c31l1n6

ceiling

c3ll4r

cellar

54un4

sauna

b4lc0ny

balcony

73rr4c3

terrace

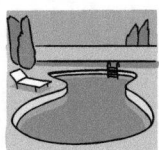

p00l

pool

l4wn m0w3r

lawn mower

5h337

sheet

b3d5pr34d

bedspread

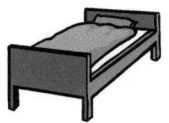

b3d

bed

br00m

broom

buck37

bucket

5w17ch

switch

l1v1n6 r00m

living room

w4llp4p3r
wallpaper
p1c7ur3
picture
l4mp
lamp
5h3lf
shelf
c4b1n37
cupboard
73l3v1510n
television
f1r3pl4c3
fireplace
fl0w3r
flower
cu5h10n
cushion
50f4
sofa
v453
vase
r3m073 c0n7r0l
remote control

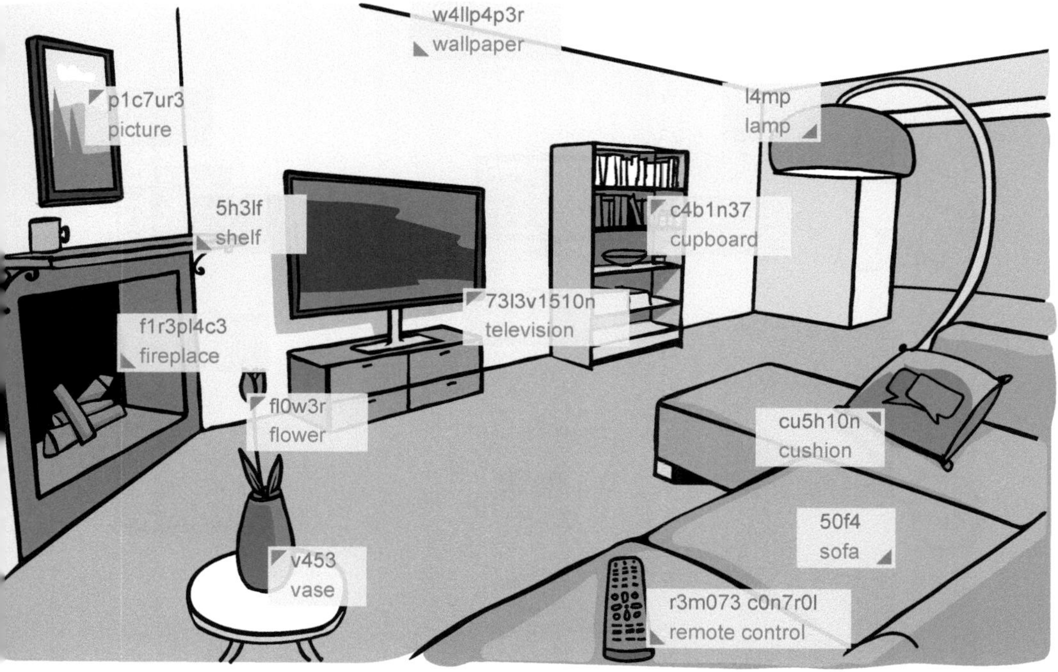

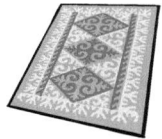

c4rp37

carpet

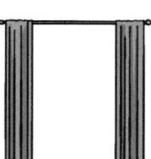

dr4p3

curtain

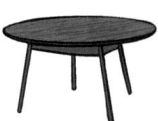

74bl3

table

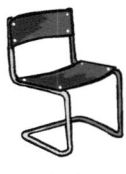

ch41r

chair

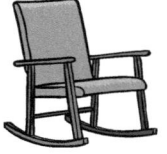

r0ck1n6 ch41r

rocking chair

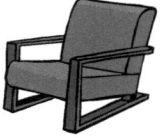

4rmch41r

armchair

b00k

book

bl4nk37

blanket

d3c0r4710n

decoration

f1r3w00d

firewood

f1lm

film

573r30 5y573m

hi-fi equipment

k3y

key

n3w5p4p3r

newspaper

p41n71n6

painting

p0573r

poster

r4d10

radio

n073b00k

notepad

v4cuum cl34n3r

hoover

c4c7u5

cactus

c4ndl3

candle

k17ch3n
kitchen

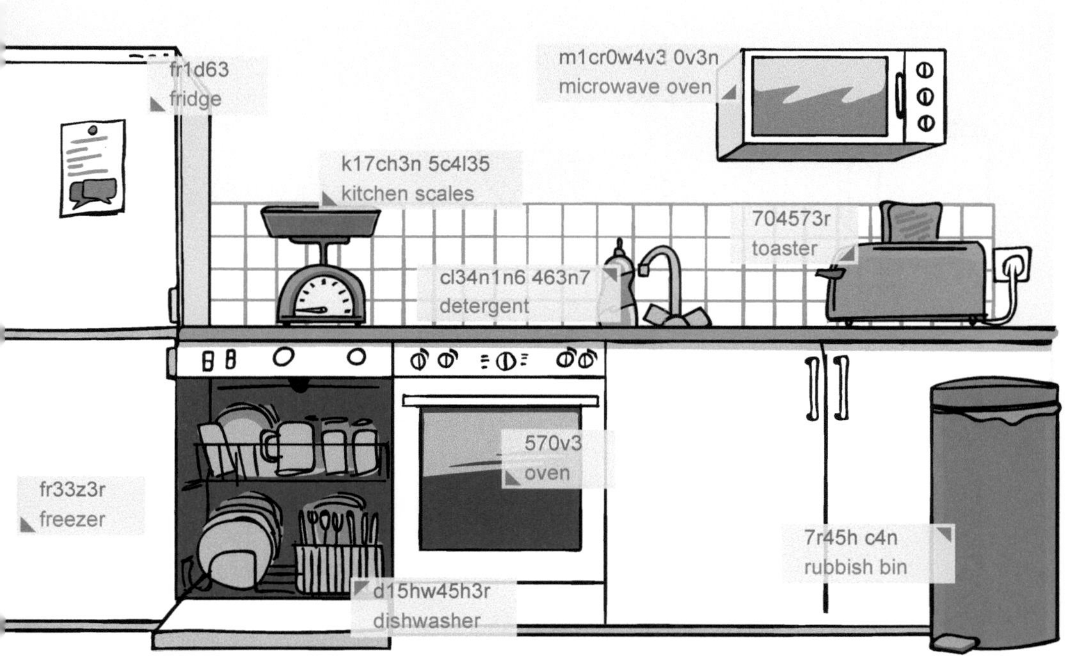
fr1d63
fridge
m1cr0w4v3 0v3n
microwave oven
k17ch3n 5c4l35
kitchen scales
704573r
toaster
cl34n1n6 463n7
detergent
570v3
oven
fr33z3r
freezer
7r45h c4n
rubbish bin
d15hw45h3r
dishwasher

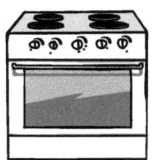

c00k3r
cooker

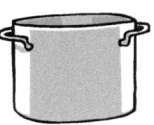

p07
pot

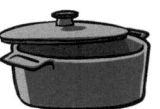

c457-1r0n p07
cast-iron pot

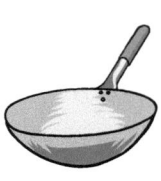

w0k / k4d41
wok / kadai

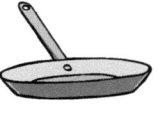

p4n
pan

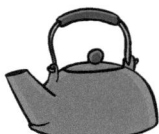

k377l3
kettle

5734m3r
....
steamer

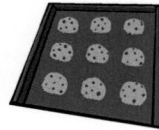

b4k1n6 7r4y
....
baking tray

cr0ck3ry
....
crockery

mu6
....
mug

b0wl
....
bowl

ch0p571ck5
....
chopsticks

l4dl3
....
ladle

5p47ul4
....
spatula

wh15k
....
whisk

57r41n3r
....
strainer

513v3
....
sieve

6r473r
....
grater

m0r74r
....
mortar

b4rb3cu3
....
barbecue

f1r3pl4c3
....
open fire

ch0pp1n6 b04rd

chopping board

r0ll1n6 p1n

rolling pin

c0rk5cr3w

corkscrew

c4n

can

c4n 0p3n3r

can opener

0v3n cl07h

pot holder

51nk

sink

bru5h

brush

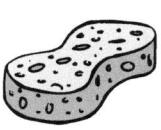

5p0n63

sponge

bl3nd3r

blender

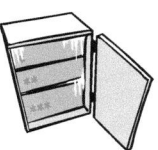

d33p fr33z3r

deep freezer

b4by b077l3

baby bottle

74p

tap

b47hr00m

bathroom

h3471n6
heating
70w3l
towel
5h0w3r
shower
5h0w3r cur741n
shower curtain
bubbl3 b47h
bubble bath
b47h7ub
bathtub
6l455
glass
w45h1n6 m4ch1n3
washing machine
74p
tap
71l35
tiles
p077y
potty
51nk
sink

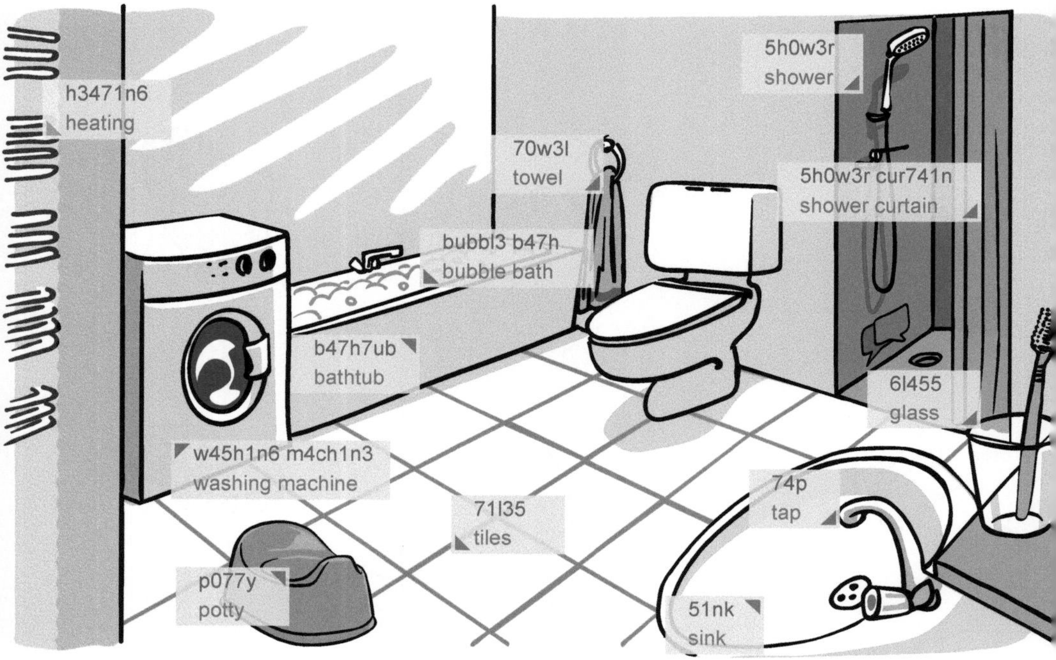

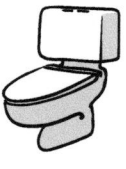

701l37

toilet

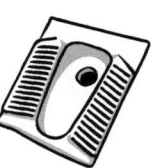

5qu47 701l37

squat toilet

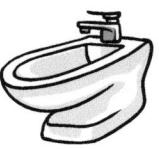

b1d37

bidet

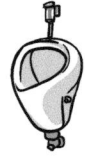

ur1n4l

urinal

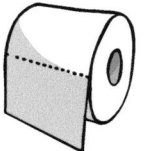

701l37 p4p3r

toilet paper

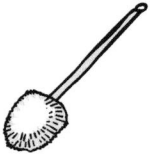

701l37 bru5h

toilet brush

7007hbru5h

toothbrush

7007hp4573

toothpaste

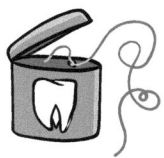

d3n74l fl055

dental floss

w45h

wash

h4nd 5h0w3r

handheld shower

d0uch3

douche

b451n

basin

b4ck bru5h

back brush

504p

soap

5h0w3r 63l

shower gel

5h4mp00

shampoo

fl4nn3l

flannel

dr41n

drain

cr3m3

cream

d30d0r4n7

deodorant

m1rr0r

mirror

h4nd m1rr0r

hand mirror

r4z0r

razor

5h4v1n6 f04m

shaving foam

4f73r5h4v3

aftershave

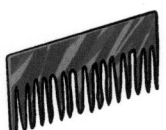

c0mb

comb

bru5h

brush

h41r-dry3r

hair dryer

h41r5pr4y

hairspray

m4k3up

makeup

l1p571ck

lipstick

n41l v4rn15h

nail varnish

c0770n w00l

cotton wool

n41l 5c1550r5

nail scissors

p3rfum3

perfume

w45hb46

washbag

5700l

stool

w316h1n6 5c4l35

weighing scale

b47hr0b3

bathrobe

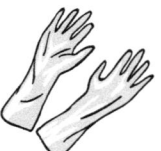

rubb3r 6l0v35

rubber gloves

74mp0n

tampon

54n174ry 70w3l

sanitary towel

ch3m1c4l 701l37

chemical toilet

ch1ld'5 r00m

child's room

4l4rm cl0ck
alarm clock
cuddly 70y
cuddly toy
70y c4r
toy car
r477l3
rattle
d0ll'5 h0u53
doll's house
pr353n7
present

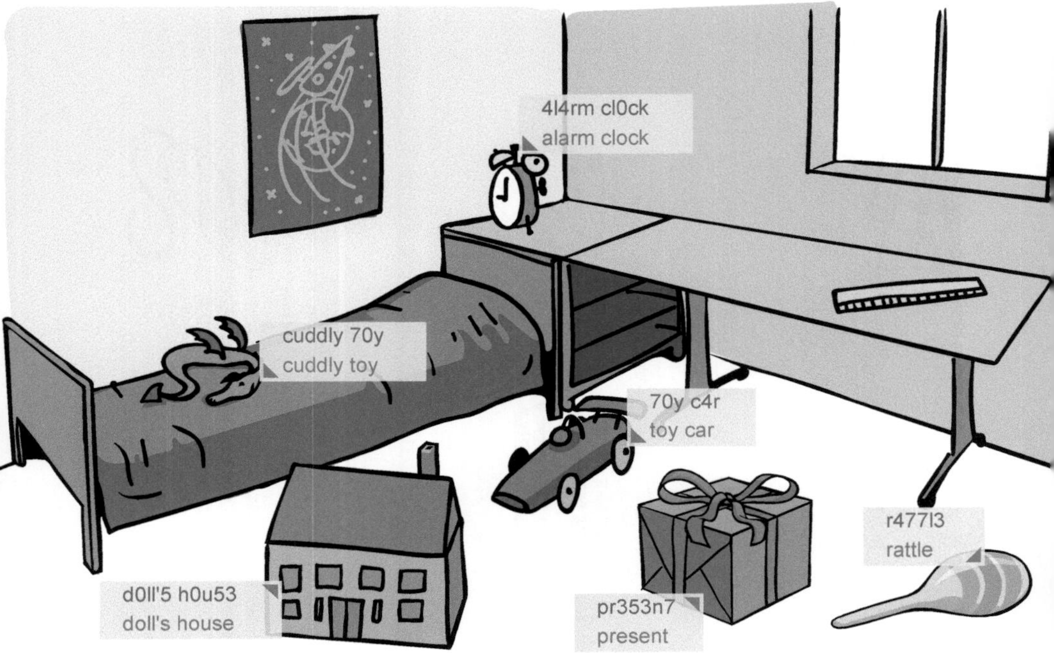

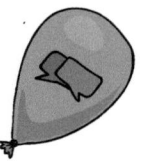

b4ll00n

balloon

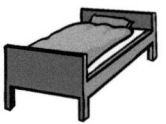

b3d

bed

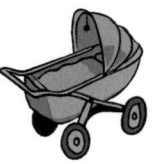

57r0ll3r

pram

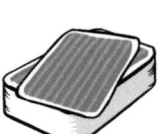

d3ck 0f c4rd5

deck of cards

j1654w

jigsaw

SUPER
MEGA

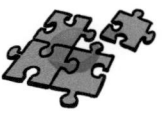

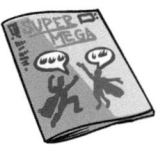

c0m1c

comic

l360 br1ck5

lego bricks

70y bl0ck5

building blocks

4c710n f16ur3

action figure

r0mp3r 5u17

babygrow

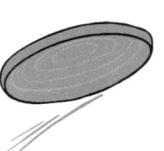

fr15b33

frisbee

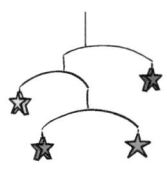

m0b1l3

mobile

b04rd 64m3

board game

d1c3

dice

m0d3l 7r41n 537

model train set

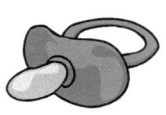

dummy

dummy

p4r7y

party

p1c7ur3 b00k

picture book

b4ll

ball

d0ll

doll

pl4y

play

54ndp17
....
sandpit

5w1n6
....
swing

70y
....
toys

v1d30 64m3 c0n50l3
....
video game console

7r1cycl3
....
tricycle

73ddy b34r
....
teddy bear

w4rdr0b3
....
wardrobe

cl07h1n6
clothing

50ck5
....
socks

570ck1n65
....
stockings

716h75
....
tights

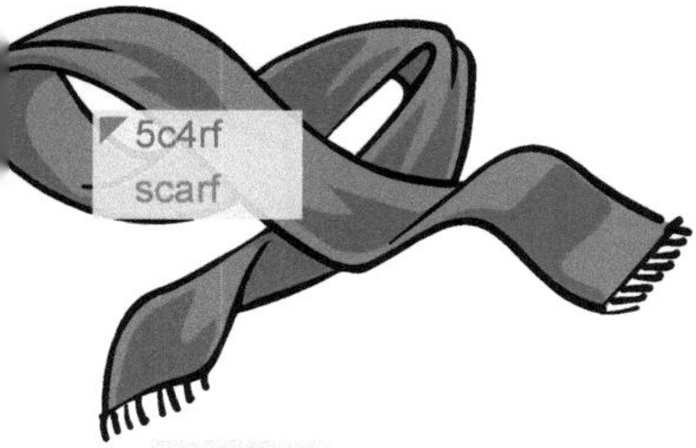

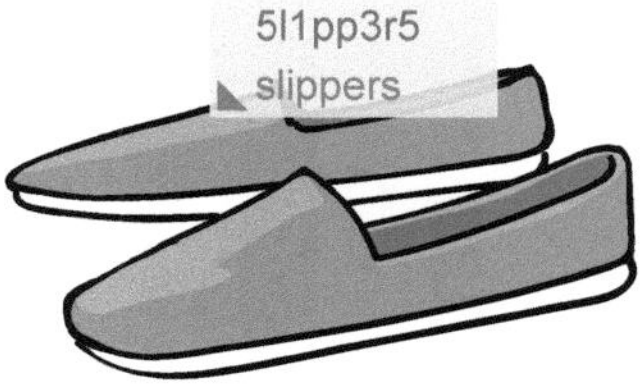

5c4rf
scarf

umbr3ll4
umbrella

7-5h1r7
t-shirt

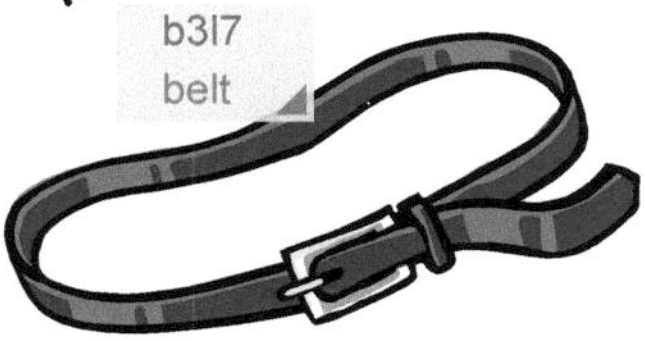

b3l7
belt

b0075
boots

5l1pp3r5
slippers

5n34k3r5
trainers

54nd4l5
sandals

5h035
shoes

rubb3r b0075
rubber boots

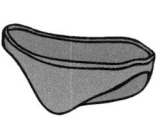

br13f5
underpants

br4
bra

und3r5h1r7
vest

cl07h1n6 - clothing

b0dy

body

p4n75

trousers

j34n5

jeans

5k1r7

skirt

bl0u53

blouse

5h1r7

shirt

pull0v3r

pullover

5w3473r

hoodie

bl4z3r

blazer

j4ck37

jacket

c047

coat

r41nc047

raincoat

c057um3

costume

dr355

dress

w3dd1n6 dr355

wedding dress

5u17

suit

n16h760wn

nightgown

p4j4m45

pyjamas

54r1

sari

h34d5c4rf

headscarf

7urb4n

turban

burk4

burqa

k4f74n

kaftan

4b4y4

abaya

5w1m5u17

swimsuit

7runk5

trunks

5h0r75

shorts

7r4ck5u17

tracksuit

4pr0n

apron

6l0v35

gloves

bu770n

button

6l45535

glasses

br4c3l37

bracelet

n3ckl4c3

necklace

r1n6

ring

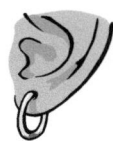

34rr1n6

earring

c4p

cap

c047 h4n63r

coat hanger

h47

hat

713

tie

z1p

zip

h3lm37

helmet

br4c35

braces

5ch00l un1f0rm

school uniform

un1f0rm

uniform

b1b
bib

dummy
dummy

d14p3r
nappy

0ff1c3
office

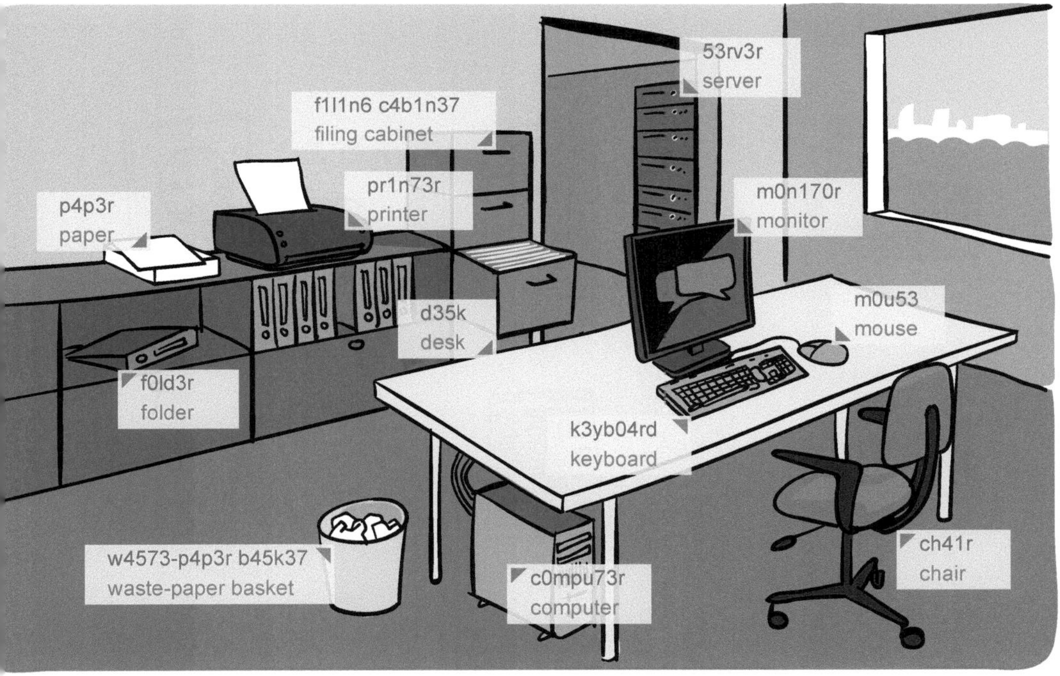

53rv3r
server

f1l1n6 c4b1n37
filing cabinet

pr1n73r
printer

m0n170r
monitor

p4p3r
paper

m0u53
mouse

d35k
desk

f0ld3r
folder

k3yb04rd
keyboard

w4573-p4p3r b45k37
waste-paper basket

c0mpu73r
computer

ch41r
chair

c0ff33 mu6
coffee mug

c4lcul470r
calculator

1n73rn37
internet

l4p70p

laptop

l3773r

letter

m355463

message

c3ll ph0n3

mobile

n37w0rk

network

ph070c0p13r

photocopier

50f7w4r3

software

73l3ph0n3

telephone

plu6 50ck37

plug socket

f4x m4ch1n3

fax machine

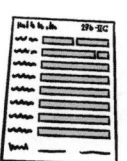

f0rm

form

d0cum3n7

document

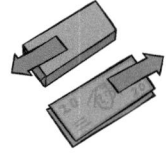

buy

buy

p4y

pay

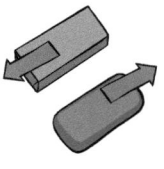

7r4d3

trade

m0n3y

money

USD

d0ll4r

dollar

EUR

3ur0

euro

JPY

y3n

yen

RUB

r0ubl3

rouble

CHF

5w155 fr4nc

Swiss franc

CNY

r3nm1nb1 yu4n

renminbi yuan

INR

rup33

rupee

c45h p01n7

cashpoint

curr3ncy 3xch4n63 0ff1c3

bureau de change

60ld

gold

51lv3r

silver

01l

oil

3n3r6y

energy

pr1c3

price

c0n7r4c7

contract

74x

tax

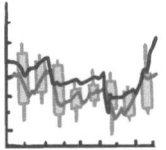

570ck

stock

w0rk

work

3mpl0y33

employee

3mpl0y3r

employer

f4c70ry

factory

5h0p

shop

0ccup4710n5

occupations

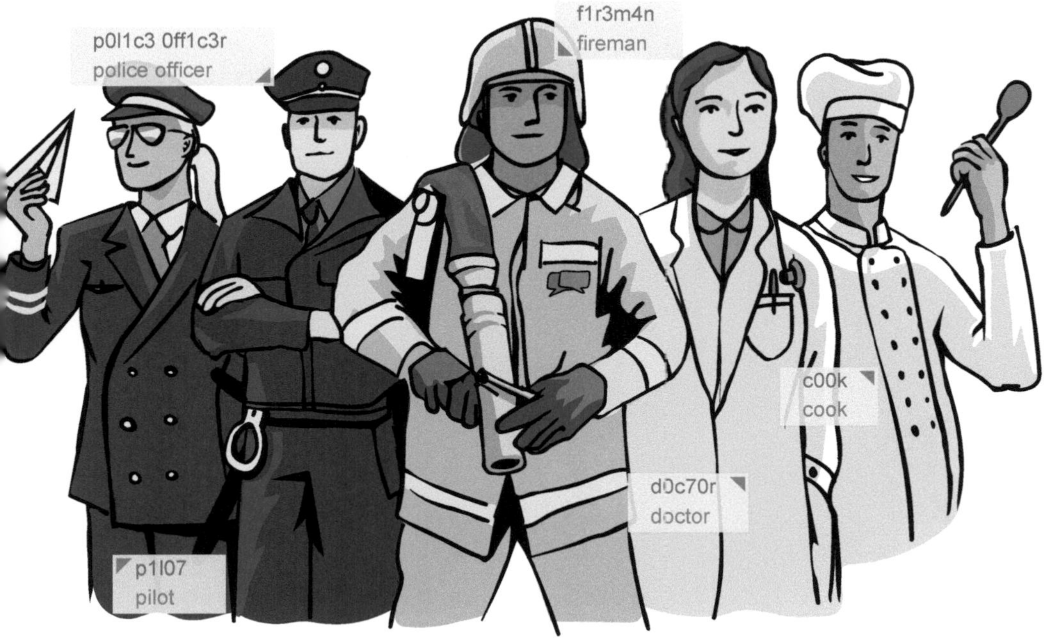
p0l1c3 0ff1c3r
police officer
f1r3m4n
fireman
c00k
cook
d0c70r
doctor
p1l07
pilot

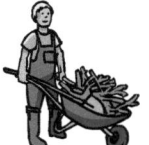

64rd3n3r

gardener

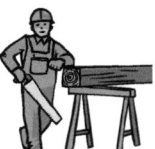

c4rp3n73r

carpenter

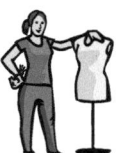

534m57r355

seamstress

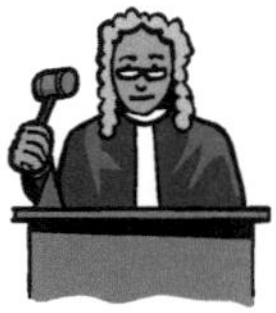

jud63

judge

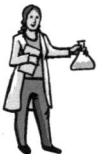

ch3m157

chemist

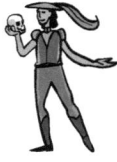

4c70r

actor

bu5 dr1v3r

bus driver

74x1 dr1v3r

taxi driver

f15h3rm4n

fisherman

cl34n1n6 l4dy

cleaning lady

r00f3r

roofer

w4173r

waiter

hun73r

hunter

p41n73r

painter

b4k3r

baker

3l3c7r1c14n

electrician

bu1ld3r

builder

3n61n33r

engineer

bu7ch3r

butcher

plumb3r

plumber

p057m4n

postman

50ld13r

soldier

4rch173c7

architect

c45h13r

cashier

fl0r157

florist

h41rdr3553r

hairdresser

c0nduc70r

conductor

m3ch4n1c

mechanic

c4p741n

captain

d3n7157

dentist

5c13n7157

scientist

r4bb1

rabbi

1m4m

imam

m0nk

monk

p4570r

clergyman

700l5

tools

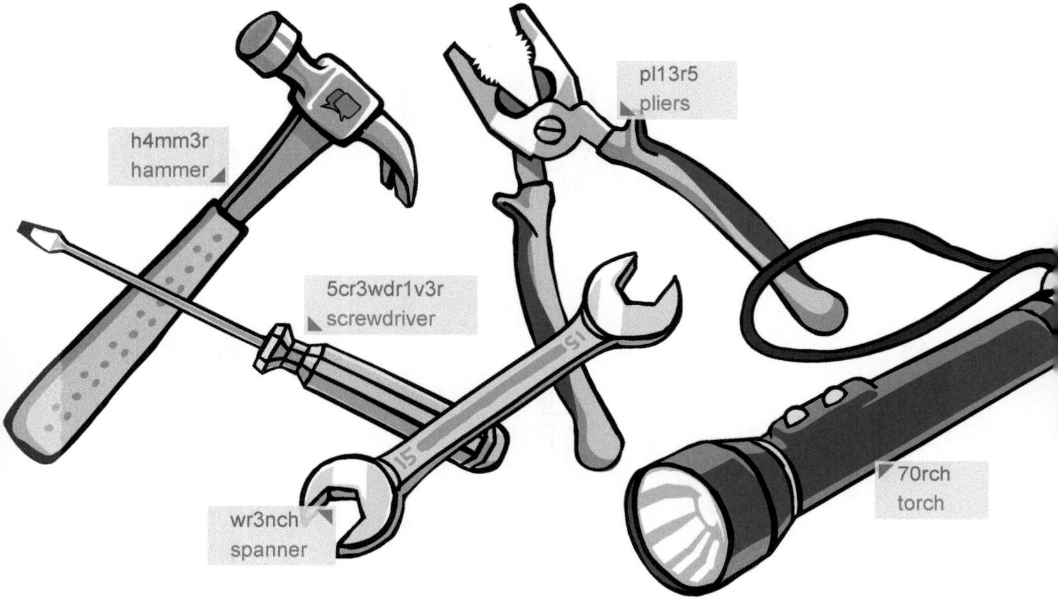
h4mm3r
hammer
pl13r5
pliers
5cr3wdr1v3r
screwdriver
wr3nch
spanner
70rch
torch

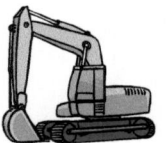

3xc4v470r

digger

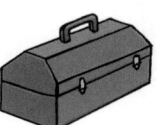

700lb0x

toolbox

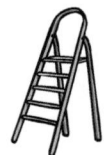

l4dd3r

ladder

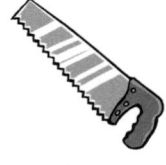

54w

saw

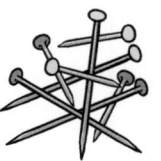

n41l5

nails

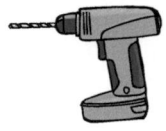

dr1ll

drill

r3p41r

repair

5h0v3l

shovel

d4mn!

Damn!

du57p4n

dustpan

p41n7 c4n

paint pot

5cr3w5

screws

mu51c4l 1n57rum3n75
musical instruments

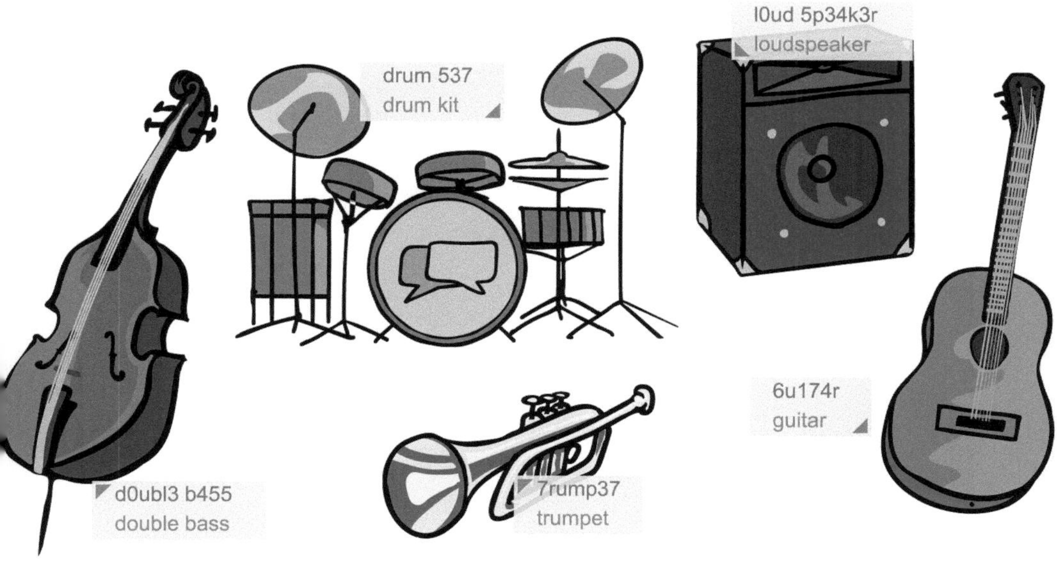

drum 537
drum kit

l0ud 5p34k3r
loudspeaker

6u174r
guitar

d0ubl3 b455
double bass

7rump37
trumpet

p14n0

piano

v10l1n

violin

b455

bass

71mp4n1

timpani

drum5

drums

k3yb04rd

keyboard

54x0ph0n3

saxophone

flu73

flute

m1cr0ph0n3

microphone

3n7r4nc3
entrance

7163r
tiger

c463
cage

z3br4
zebra

4n1m4l f33d
animal feed

p4nd4
panda

4n1m4l5

animals

3l3ph4n7

elephant

k4n64r00

kangaroo

rh1n0

rhino

60r1ll4

gorilla

b34r

bear

c4m3l

camel

057r1ch

ostrich

l10n

lion

m0nk3y

monkey

fl4m1n60

flamingo

p4rr07

parrot

p0l4r b34r

polar bear

p3n6u1n

penguin

5h4rk

shark

p34c0ck

peacock

5n4k3

snake

cr0c0d1l3

crocodile

z00k33p3r

zookeeper

534l

seal

j46u4r

jaguar

z00 - zoo

p0ny

pony

l30p4rd

leopard

h1pp0

hippo

61r4ff3

giraffe

346l3

eagle

b04r

boar

f15h

fish

7ur7l3

turtle

w4lru5

walrus

f0x

fox

64z3ll3

gazelle

z00 - zoo

4m3r1c4n f007b4ll
American football

cycl1n6
cycling

73nn15
tennis

b45k37b4ll
basketball

5w1mm1n6
swimming

1c3 h0ck3y
ice hockey

b0x1n6
boxing

50cc3r

football

b4dm1n70n

badminton

47hl371c5

athletics

h4ndb4ll

handball

5k11n6

skiing

p0l0

polo

4c71v17135
activities

l4u6h
laugh
jump
jump
hu6
hug
w4lk
walk
51n6
sing
dr34m
dream
pr4y
pray
k155
kiss

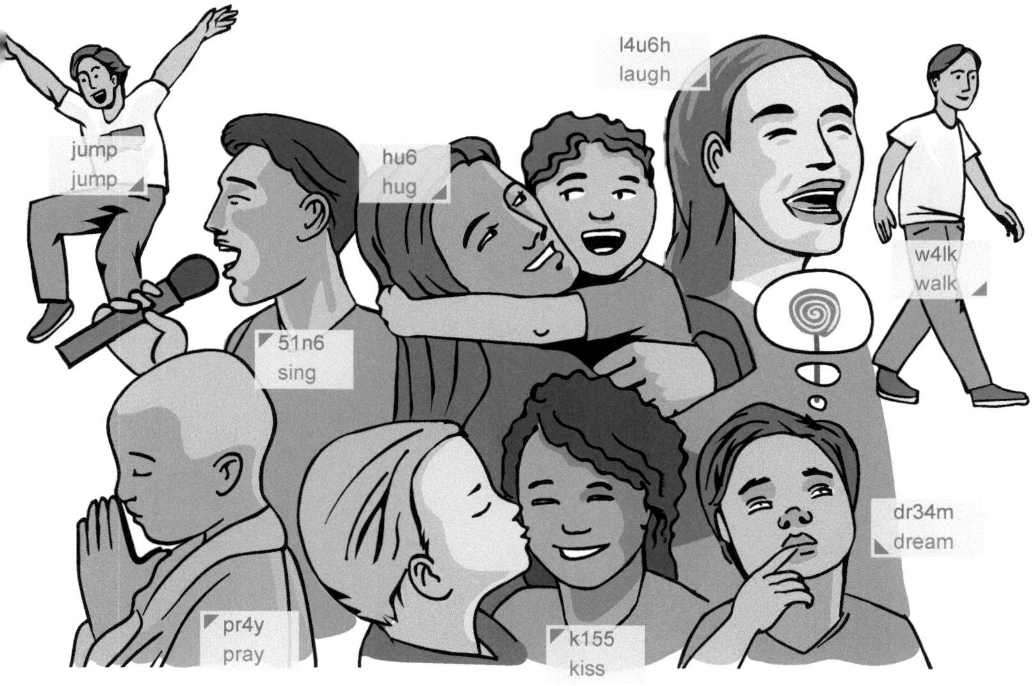

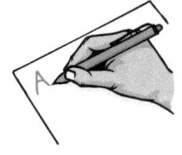

wr173

write

dr4w

draw

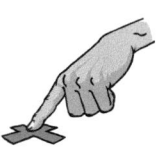

5h0w

show

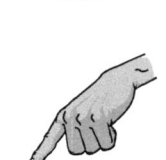

pu5h

push

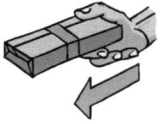

61v3

give

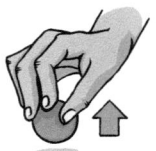

74k3

take

h4v3

have

d0

do

b3

be

574nd

stand

run

run

pull

pull

7hr0w

throw

f4ll

fall

l13

lie

w417

wait

c4rry

carry

517

sit

637 dr3553d

get dressed

5l33p

sleep

w4k3 up

wake up

l00k 47

look at

cry

cry

57r0k3

stroke

c0mb

comb

74lk

talk

und3r574nd

understand

45k

ask

l1573n

listen

dr1nk

drink

347

eat

71dy up

tidy up

l0v3

love

c00k

cook

dr1v3

drive

fly

fly

5411
sail

c4lcul473
calculate

r34d
read

l34rn
learn

w0rk
work

m4rry
marry

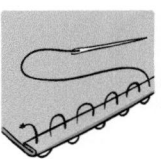

53w
sew

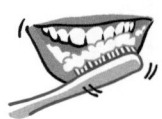

bru5h 7337h
brush teeth

k1ll
kill

5m0k3
smoke

53nd
send

f4m1ly
family

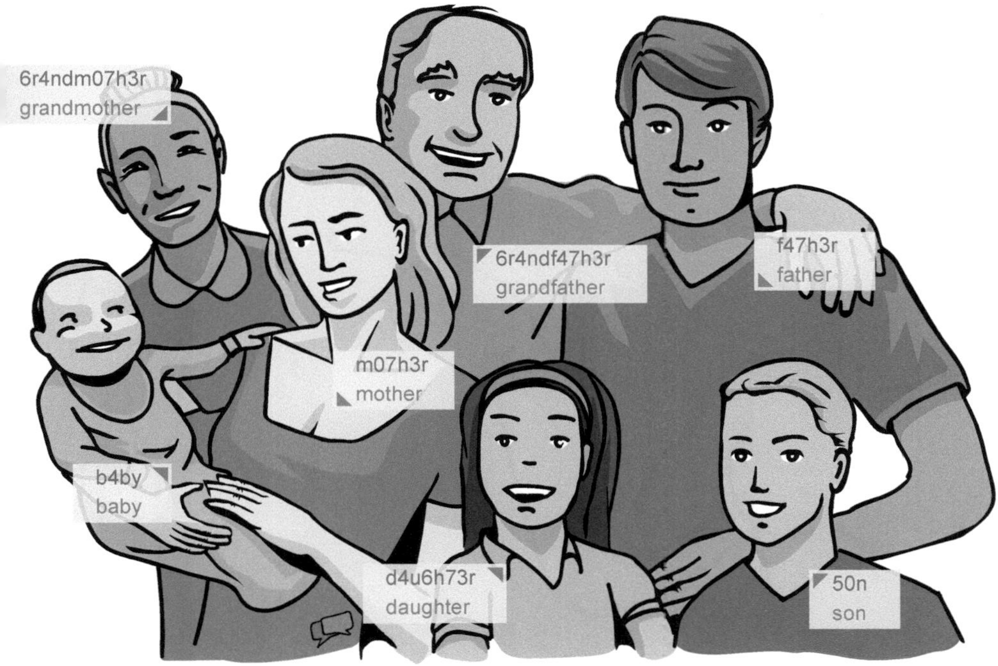
6r4ndm07h3r
grandmother
6r4ndf47h3r
grandfather
f47h3r
father
m07h3r
mother
b4by
baby
d4u6h73r
daughter
50n
son

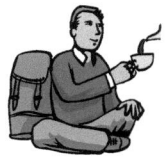

6u357

guest

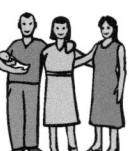

4un7

aunt

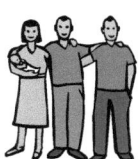

uncl3

uncle

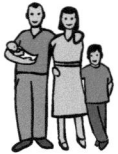

br07h3r

brother

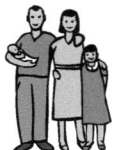

51573r

sister

b0dy

body

f0r3h34d
forehead
3y3
eye
5h0uld3r
shoulder
f1n63r
finger
f4c3
face
ch1n
chin
h4nd
hand
l36
leg
br3457
breast
4rm
arm

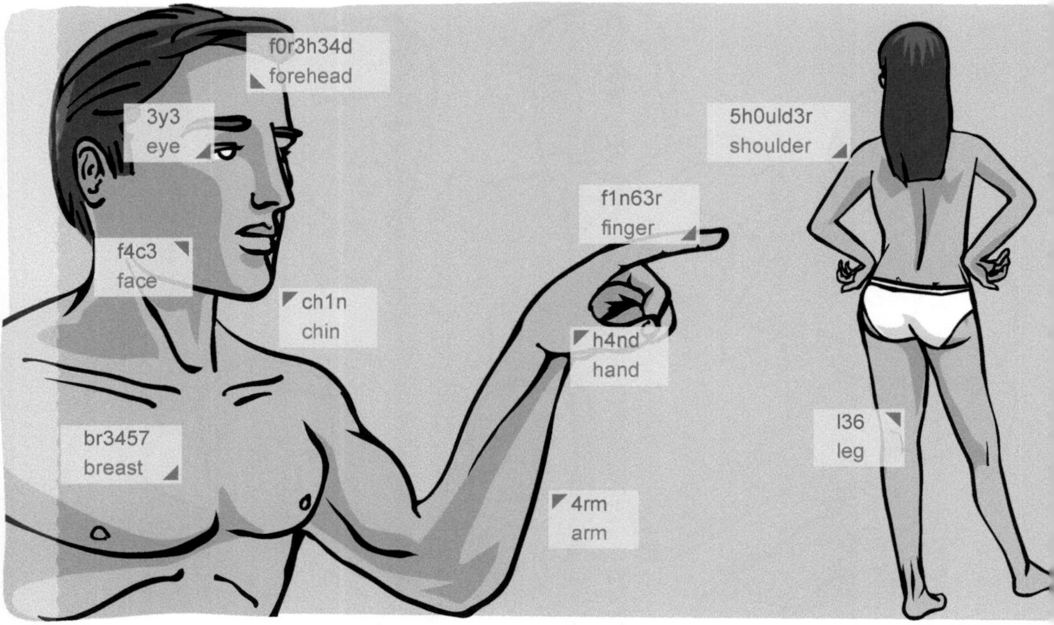

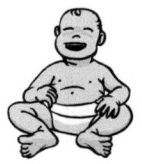

b4by

baby

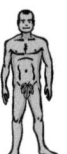

m4n

man

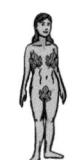

w0m4n

woman

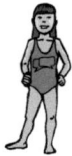

61rl

girl

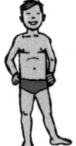

b0y

boy

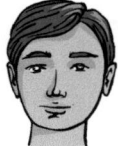

h34d

head

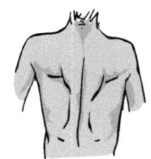

b4ck

back

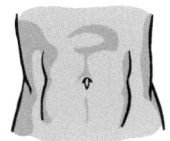

b3lly

belly

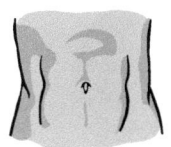

n4v3l

belly button

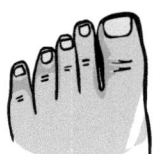

703

toe

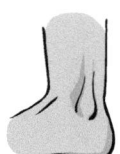

h33l

heel

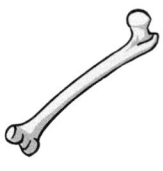

b0n3

bone

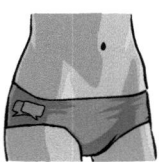

h1p

hip

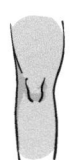

kn33

knee

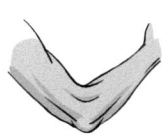

3lb0w

elbow

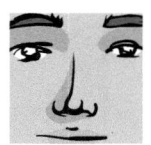

n053

nose

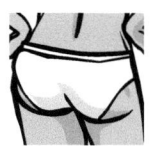

bu770ck5

bottom

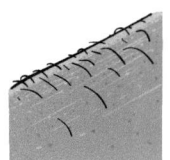

5k1n

skin

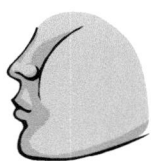

ch33k

cheek

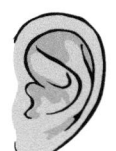

34r

ear

l1p

lip

m0u7h

mouth

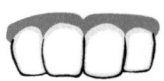

7007h

tooth

70n6u3

tongue

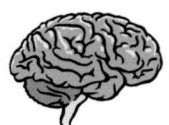

br41n

brain

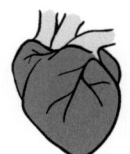

h34r7

heart

mu5cl3

muscle

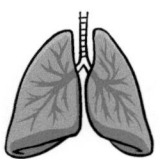

lun6

lung

l1v3r

liver

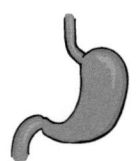

570m4ch

stomach

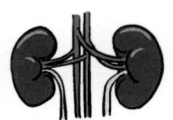

k1dn3y5

kidneys

53x

sex

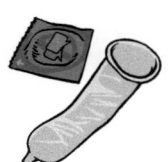

c0nd0m

condom

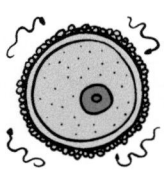

0vum

ovum

53m3n

semen

pr36n4ncy

pregnancy

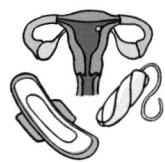

m3n57ru4710n

menstruation

v461n4

vagina

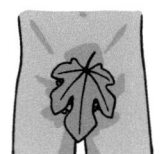

p3n15

penis

3y3br0w

eyebrow

h41r

hair

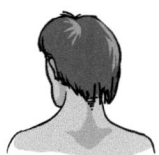

n3ck

neck

b0dy - body

h05p174l

hospital

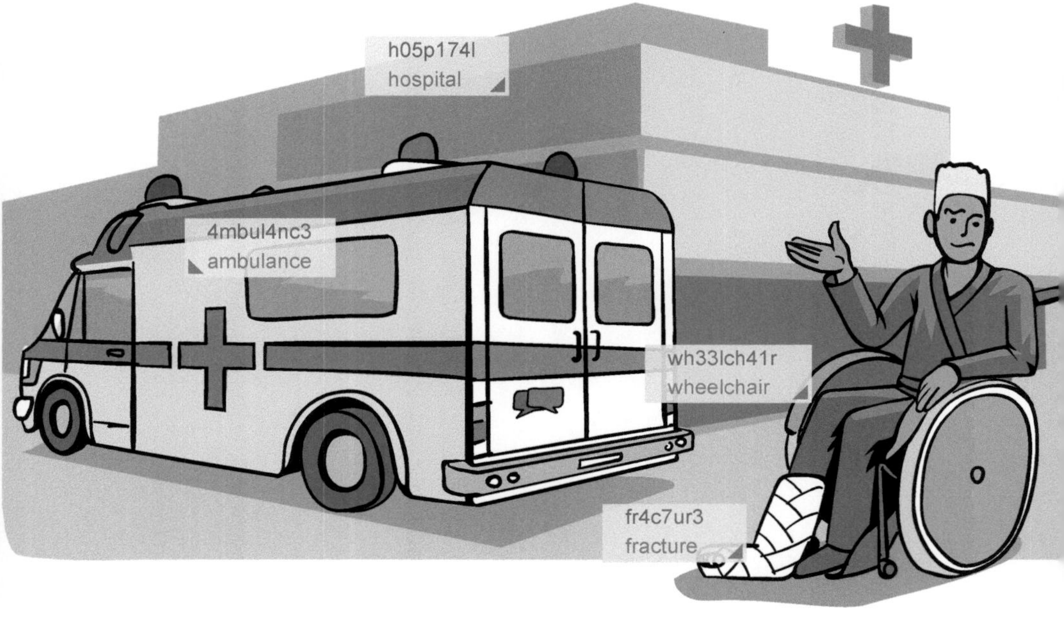

h05p174l
hospital
4mbul4nc3
ambulance
wh33lch41r
wheelchair
fr4c7ur3
fracture

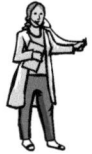

d0c70r

doctor

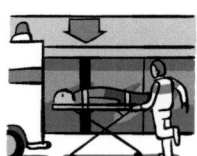

3m3r63ncy r00m

emergency room

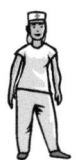

nur53

nurse

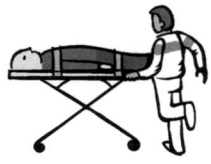

3m3r63ncy

emergency

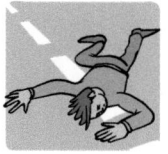

unc0n5c10u5

unconscious

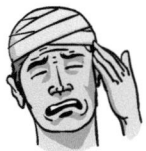

p41n

pain

1njury

injury

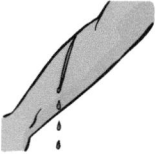

bl33d1n6

bleeding

h34r7 4774ck

heart attack

57r0k3

stroke

4ll3r6y

allergy

c0u6h

cough

f3v3r

fever

flu

flu

d14rrh34

diarrhoea

h34d4ch3

headache

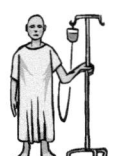

c4nc3r

cancer

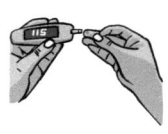

d14b3735

diabetes

5ur630n

surgeon

5c4lp3l

scalpel

0p3r4710n

operation

c7

CT

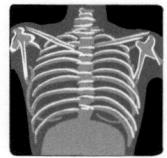

x-r4y

x-ray

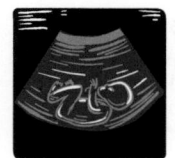

ul7r450und

ultrasound

f4c3 m45k

face mask

d153453

disease

w4171n6 r00m

waiting room

cru7ch

crutch

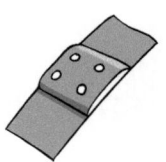

pl4573r

plaster

b4nd463

bandage

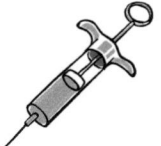

1nj3c710n

injection

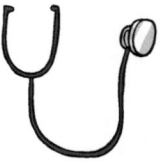

5737h05c0p3

stethoscope

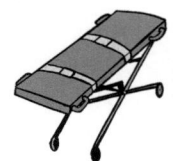

57r37ch3r

stretcher

cl1n1c4l 7h3rm0m373r

clinical thermometer

b1r7h

birth

0v3rw316h7

overweight

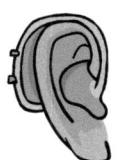

h34r1n6 41d

hearing aid

d151nf3c74n7

disinfectant

1nf3c710n

infection

v1ru5

virus

h1v / 41d5

HIV / AIDS

m3d1c1n3

medicine

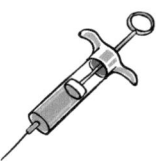

v4cc1n4710n

vaccination

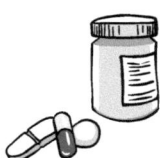

74bl375

tablets

p1ll

pill

3m3r63ncy c4ll

emergency call

bl00d pr355ur3 m0n170r

blood pressure monitor

1ll / h34l7hy

ill / healthy

h3lp!

Help!

4l4rm

alarm

4554ul7

assault

4774ck

attack

d4n63r

danger

3m3r63ncy 3x17

emergency exit

f1r3!

Fire!

f1r3 3x71n6u15h3r

fire extinguisher

4cc1d3n7

accident

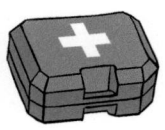

f1r57-41d k17

first-aid kit

505

SOS

p0l1c3

police

3ur0p3

Europe

n0r7h 4m3r1c4

North America

50u7h 4m3r1c4

South America

4fr1c4

Africa

4514

Asia

4u57r4l14

Australia

47l4n71c

Atlantic

p4c1f1c

Pacific

1nd14n 0c34n

Indian Ocean

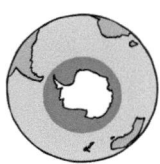

4n74rc71c 0c34n

Antarctic Ocean

4rc71c 0c34n

Arctic Ocean

n0r7h p0l3

North Pole

50u7h p0l3

South Pole

4n74rc71c4

Antarctica

34r7h

Earth

l4nd

land

534

sea

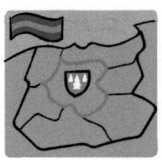

15l4nd

island

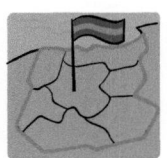

n4710n

nation

57473

state

cl0ck f4c3

clock face

h0ur h4nd

hour hand

m1nu73 h4nd

minute hand

53c0nd h4nd

second hand

wh47 71m3 15 17?

What time is it?

d4y

day

71m3

time

n0w

now

d16174l w47ch

digital watch

m1nu73

minute

h0ur

hour

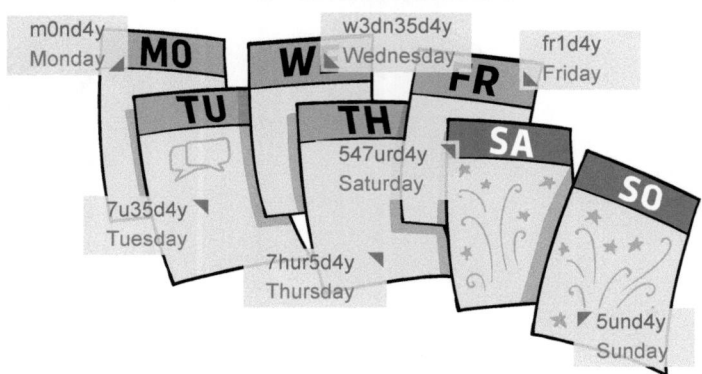

m0nd4y
Monday

w3dn35d4y
Wednesday

fr1d4y
Friday

7u35d4y
Tuesday

547urd4y
Saturday

7hur5d4y
Thursday

5und4y
Sunday

y3573rd4y

yesterday

70d4y

today

70m0rr0w

tomorrow

m0rn1n6

morning

n00n

noon

3v3n1n6

evening

w0rkd4y5

business days

w33k3nd

weekend

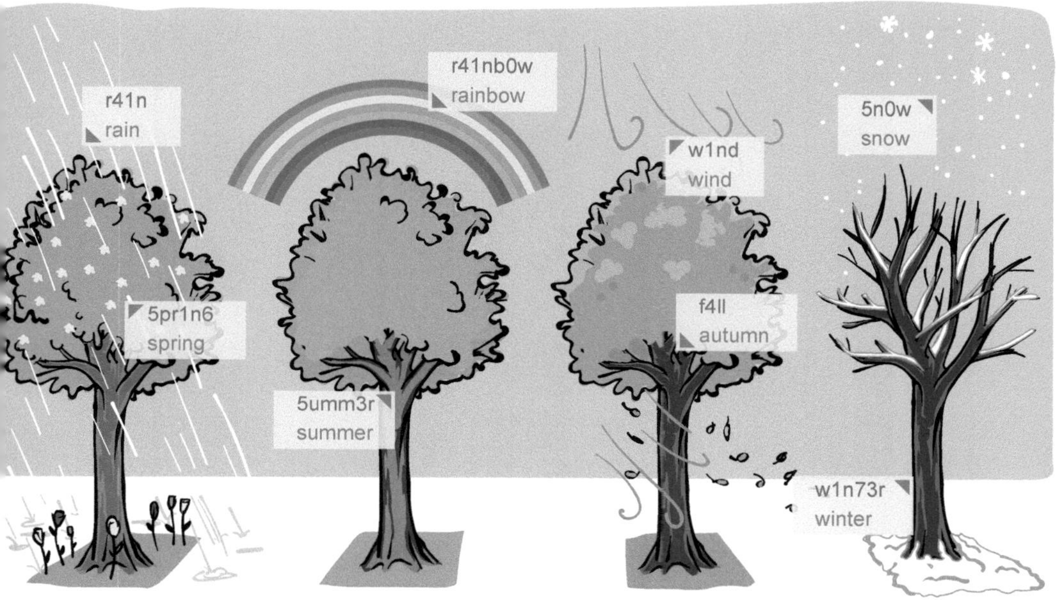

r41n
rain

r41nb0w
rainbow

5n0w
snow

w1nd
wind

5pr1n6
spring

f4ll
autumn

5umm3r
summer

w1n73r
winter

w347h3r f0r3c457
....
weather forecast

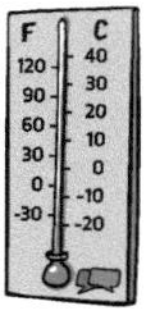

7h3rm0m373r
....
thermometer

5un5h1n3
....
sunshine

cl0ud
....
cloud

f06
....
fog

hum1d17y
....
humidity

l16h7n1n6

lightning

7hund3r

thunder

570rm

storm

h41l

hail

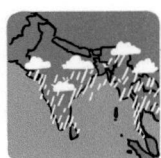

m0n500n

monsoon

fl00d

flood

1c3

ice

j4nu4ry

January

f3bru4ry

February

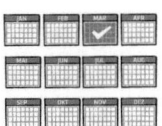

m4rch

March

4pr1l

April

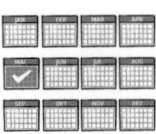

m4y

May

jun3

June

july

July

4u6u57

August

53p73mb3r

September

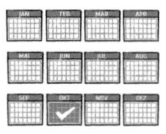

0c70b3r

October

n0v3mb3r

November

d3c3mb3r

December

c1rcl3

circle

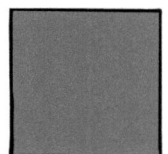

5qu4r3

square

r3c74n6l3

rectangle

7r14n6l3

triangle

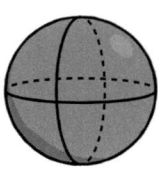

5ph3r3

sphere

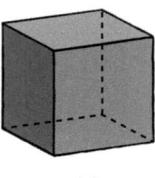

cub3

cube

wh173

white

y3ll0w

yellow

0r4n63

orange

p1nk

pink

r3d

red

purpl3

purple

blu3

blue

6r33n

green

br0wn

brown

6r4y

grey

bl4ck

black

4 l07 / 4 l177l3

a lot / a little

4n6ry / c4lm

angry / calm

b34u71ful / u6ly

beautiful / ugly

b361nn1n6 / 3nd

beginning / end

b16 / 5m4ll

big / small

br16h7 / d4rk

bright / dark

br07h3r / 51573r

brother / sister

cl34n / d1r7y

clean / dirty

c0mpl373 / 1nc0mpl373

complete / incomplete

d4y / n16h7

day / night

d34d / 4l1v3

dead / alive

w1d3 / n4rr0w

wide / narrow

3d1bl3 / 1n3d1bl3

edible / inedible

3v1l / k1nd

evil / kind

3xc173d / b0r3d

excited / bored

f47 / 7h1n

fat / thin

f1r57 / l457

first / last

fr13nd / 3n3my

friend / enemy

full / 3mp7y

full / empty

h4rd / 50f7

hard / soft

h34vy / l16h7

heavy / light

hun63r / 7h1r57

hunger / thirst

1ll / h34l7hy

ill / healthy

1ll364l / l364l

illegal / legal

1n73ll163n7 / 57up1d

intelligent / stupid

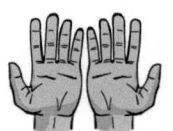

l3f7 / r16h7

left / right

n34r / f4r

near / far

n3w / u53d
....
new / used

n07h1n6 / 50m37h1n6
....
nothing / something

0ld / y0un6
....
old / young

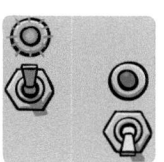

0n / 0ff
....
on / off

0p3n / cl053d
....
open / closed

qu137 / l0ud
....
quiet / loud

r1ch / p00r
....
rich / poor

r16h7 / wr0n6
....
right / wrong

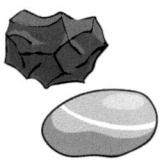

r0u6h / 5m007h
....
rough / smooth

54d / h4ppy
....
sad / happy

5h0r7 / l0n6
....
short / long

5l0w / f457
....
slow / fast

w37 / dry
....
wet / dry

w4rm / c00l
....
warm / cool

w4r / p34c3
....
war / peace

0

z3r0

zero

1

0n3

one

2

7w0

two

3

7hr33

three

4

f0ur

four

5

f1v3

five

6

51x

six

7

53v3n

seven

8

316h7

eight

9

n1n3

nine

10

73n

ten

11

3l3v3n

eleven

12

7w3lv3

twelve

13

7h1r733n

thirteen

14

f0ur733n

fourteen

15

f1f733n

fifteen

16

51x733n

sixteen

17

53v3n733n

seventeen

18

316h733n

eighteen

19

n1n3733n

nineteen

20

7w3n7y

twenty

100

hundr3d

hundred

1.000

7h0u54nd

thousand

1.000.000

m1ll10n

million

3n6l15h

English

4m3r1c4n 3n6l15h

American English

ch1n353 m4nd4r1n

Chinese Mandarin

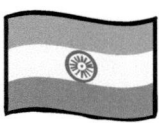

h1nd1

Hindi

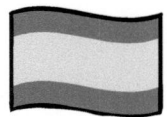

5p4n15h

Spanish

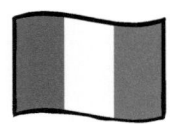

fr3nch

French

4r4b1c

Arabic

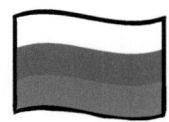

ru5514n

Russian

p0r7u6u353

Portuguese

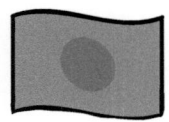

b3n64l1

Bengali

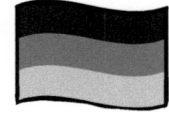

63rm4n

German

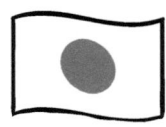

j4p4n353

Japanese

1

I

y0u

you

h3 / 5h3 / 17

he / she / it

w3

we

y0u

you

7h3y

they

wh0?

who?

wh47?

what?

h0w?

how?

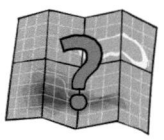

wh3r3?

where?

wh3n?

when?

n4m3

name

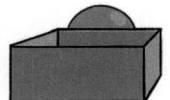

b3h1nd

behind

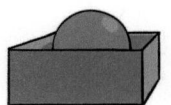

1n

in

1n fr0n7 0f

in front of

0v3r

over

0n

on

und3r

under

b351d3

beside

b37w33n

between

pl4c3

place